Praise for *John Owen on Pastoral Preaching*

"What you have in this book is a survey of John Owen's writings . . . which serves to provide the reader with a clear and concise introduction to the mind and heart of Owen on pastoral preaching. Miller highlights for the church a key historical example of how faithful pastors are to regard the sacred duty of proclaiming the word of God to the people of God."

—WILL BARNETT, Lead Pastor, First Southern Baptist Church

"Miller's examination and explanation of the writings of John Owen on preaching in the context of pastoral ministry is a reminder to us . . . that the church and her shepherds must return to the simple yet weighty task of preaching the word. Through Owen's works, Miller shows us that nothing but the word preached will change hearts and sanctify God's people. . . . Miller's book is a timely and welcome reminder to return to such simplicity!"

—JOSH WILSON, Pastor, First Baptist Church Park Hills

"Though John Owen is one of the church's foremost theologians, his primary commitment was not to the academy but to the church. Persuaded that the word is the inspired word, Owen was convinced that pastoral preaching was his chief privilege and responsibility. Every pastor, especially those, like myself, who love John Owen, should read this excellent and insightful book on the nature and primacy of the pastor's week-to-week pulpit ministry!"

—JEFFREY D. JOHNSON, President, Grace Bible Theological Seminary

"In a day when pastoral preaching has fallen from prominence in the evangelical church, Justin Miller's work here points back to its previous centrality. May the Lord use examples like John Owen to restore preaching to its proper place in the church!"

—SAM WALDRON, President, Covenant Baptist Theological Seminary

John Owen on
Pastoral Preaching

John Owen on Pastoral Preaching

JUSTIN MILLER

WIPF & STOCK · Eugene, Oregon

JOHN OWEN ON PASTORAL PREACHING

Wipf & Stock
An Imprint of Wipf and Stock Publishers
199 W. 8th Ave., Suite 3
Eugene, OR 97401

www.wipfandstock.com

PAPERBACK ISBN: 978-1-6667-3309-9
HARDCOVER ISBN: 978-1-6667-2740-1
EBOOK ISBN: 978-1-6667-2741-8

11/30/21

To Christ my King. All wanes in comparison and all is but rags in view of your glory. My heart is yours forever.

To my wife JoDawn, your love for Christ and encouragement in this endeavor pushed me forward.

To my kids, I pray that you see, savor, and walk with the King of Glory all your days.

To Dr. Benge, thank you for your encouragement, wisdom, and insight in this endeavor as well as in pastoral ministry.

To my church family, God has been so kind to allow me to serve as an elder amongst a people who love Christ dearly from His Word.

Contents

Contents

Introduction to John Owen

THOSE WHO DO NOT learn from history are doomed to repeat it.[1] This statement is often used to express the importance of a historical understanding of humanity and its progress, or lack thereof, and has been the battle cry for many educators emphasizing the importance of an education in history to prevent a repeat of past historical mistakes and atrocities. However, history does more than just remind us of past failures to avoid; it illuminates to us past examples to be followed. One possible example in the arena of Biblical thought and practice is John Owen.

John Owen, the dissenter and theologian, occupied a prominent place in the proclamation of the gospel in seventeenth-century England until his death on August 24, 1683, at sixty-seven years old.[2] Why study John Owen? J. I. Packer once argued that we all need to read the Puritans (John Owen is one) for we are spiritual dwarfs in comparison to them.[3] Packer also called John Owen a "Puritan colossus and perhaps the best theologian England ever produced."[4] Carl Trueman wrote, "Owen was without a doubt the most significant intellect in England in the third quarter of the seventeenth century."[5] The literature John Owen produced, the doctrines he defended, and the life he lived has profoundly shaped

1. This is a quote often attributed to writer and philosopher George Santayana.

2. See Thomson's *Life of John Owen* in Owen, *Works*, 1:cxiv.

3. Packer, *Quest for Godliness*, quoted in Barrett and Haykin, *Owen on the Christian Life*, 18.

4. Packer, quoted in Cooper, *John Owen*, 12.

5. Trueman, *John Owen*, 1.

others' understanding of Christ's gospel and faithfulness to it. His understanding of the cross of Christ and the pursuit of holiness, as well as his passionate defense of the doctrines of grace, impacted his generation and others to come. Men committed to Biblical truth like John Owen are historical examples that are helpful to glean from with the intention of repeating the historical example of their lives in Christ, for the glory of God and the good of his church.

John Owen is well-known today mostly for his writings, which were numerous and spread over forty years.[6] One historian described Owen's writing style as daunting in their complexity and in their style, with sentences frequently long, perplexed, and encumbered with adjectives, often selected without great care of helpful grammatical structure.[7] He wrote on the major themes of Calvinism, true Catholic orthodoxy, church polity, and the pursuit of holiness.[8] John Owen's accomplishments as a scholar are highlighted, and his writing on the mortification of sin and the atonement of Christ emphasized. Yet, John Owen was also a churchman who sought to see the visible church refined, which he defined as "universality of men professing the doctrine of the Gospel and obedience to God in Christ, according to it, throughout the world."[9] His view of the pastoral preaching ministry of a called man of God perhaps is just as helpful as his theological writings for those who wish to understand what faithfulness to Christ as a preaching pastor is, as well as looks like. Owen outlined with great Biblical clarity the high call of preaching to a local church. His passion for pastors to preach the Word rightly and execute their ministry faithfully is undeniable. One great example of this is his strong and bold statement in his book on the *True Nature of a Gospel Church* whereby he states:

> The first principle duty of a pastor is to feed the flock by diligent preaching of the Word. It is a promise relating to the new testament, that God would give unto his church 'pastors according to his own heart, which should feed

6. Elswell, *Evangelical Dictionary of Theology*, 877.

7. Cooper, *John Owen*, 5.

8. Elswell, *Evangelical Dictionary of Theology*, 877.

9. Owen, *Works*, 13:137.

them with knowledge and understanding,' Jer. Iii.15. This
by teaching or preaching the word, and no otherwise.
This feeding is of the essence of the office of a pastor, as
unto exercise of it; so that he who doth not, or cannot, or
will not feed the flock is no pastor, whatever outward call
or work may have in the church.[10]

John Owen, from his statement, believed the prime duty of a
pastor was to feed the flock the word of God week in and week out.
To expound to them the truth of the Scriptures. This primary duty
was not to be neglected and was to be performed with the utmost
diligence and care. Owen's statements mirror, it appears, the Biblical charge of Jesus to Peter in John 21 as well as Paul to Timothy in
2 Tim 4:1–6.

John Owen later in the same book went on to state the pastoral
office's function and role, which he defined as the duties of "prayer,"
"the administration of the seals," "preservation of the truth," and
"the care of the people's souls under his charge."[11] In his book *True
Nature of a Gospel Church*, as well as his sermons and other books,
he took great pains to convey the role of a pastor with regards to
the local flock in which the Lord Jesus had entrusted to his care.
This book will endeavor to evaluate John Owen's view of pastoral
preaching by comparing Owen's writings on the subject to the clear
admonitions in Holy Scripture on this subject matter. The aim is to
discern if Owen's view of the pastoral ministry reflected the Scriptural admonitions rightly. To do this there are three areas of analysis
this book will emphasize with regards to pastoral preaching and
Owen's thought on pastoral preaching. First, we will analyze Owen's
understanding of the recipients of pastoral preaching with particular focus on how that shaped his approach to preaching. Next, we
will examine the priority of pastoral preaching per Owen particularly in light of Paul's imperative to Timothy in 2 Tim 4:1–2. Lastly,
this book will endeavor to analyze Owen's understanding of pastoral
preaching in all its aspects with Holy Scripture as the measurement
of faithfulness. Before beginning these specific areas of analysis, it

10. Owen, *Works*, 16:74–75.
11. Barret and Haykin, *Owen on the Christian Life*, 77–88.

is helpful to first understand a little of the life and times of John Owen to give a perspective concerning his thought on the pastoral preaching ministry. It is necessary to study his writings on pastoral preaching considering his context to better grasp what he is saying.

John Owen's Life and Ministry

John Owen was born in 1616 in Stadhampton, Oxfordshire.[12] His father was a puritan pastor of the local parish church.[13] He studied theology and classics at Queen's College, Oxford, graduating with his Bachelor of Arts in 1632 when he was sixteen and with his Master of Arts when he was nineteen on April 27, 1635.[14] Due to the tumultuous movements occurring in the academic world at the time (namely, the Archbishop of Canterbury seeking to purge nonconformist ideals), Owen took on a chaplain role before he eventually was called to his first pastorate and parish.[15] His first parish was at Fordham in Essex in 1642 where he pastored while the English nation was engulfed in civil war.[16] Some believe it was at this church that he began to move to a more congregationalist approach with regards to church government in contrast to his presbyterian upbringing.[17] In 1646–47 his second pastorate was at Fordham, a secluded village in a lowly populated rural region.[18] He saw his charge more as the pastor of a congregation rather than a parish mindset, and it was during this time that he preached to parliament for the first time with many more preaching opportunities to come before parliament.[19] In 1646 it was at the age of thirty that Owen preached a message before the House of Commons in St. Margaret's Church,

12. Douglas and Comfort, *Who's Who in Christian History*, 525.

13. Barret and Haykin, *Owen on the Christian Life*, 23.

14. Barret and Haykin, *Owen on the Christian Life*, 23.

15. Barret and Haykin, *Owen on the Christian Life*, 23.

16. Douglas and Comfort, *Who's Who in Christian History*, 525.

17. Elswell, *Evangelical Dictionary of Theology*, 877.

18. See Thomson's *Life of John Owen* in Owen, *Works*, 1:xxxiii.

19. Cross and and Livingstone, *Oxford Dictionary of the Christian Church*, 1210–11.

Westminster.[20] It was a sermon on the propagation of the gospel in all parts of Britain. His fame grew from this point on.[21] It was also during this time period that he accompanied Cromwell with parliament's armies to Scotland and then to Ireland.[22] After the civil war in England ended in 1648, John Owen took up the position of chaplain for Oliver Cromwell, when in 1649 Cromwell returned to Ireland.[23] Later in 1650 Owen was appointed preacher of the state and a chaplain to Cromwell in Cromwell's endeavors in Scotland.[24]

John Owen was later appointed to the prestigious position of dean of Christ's Church at Oxford University in 1651, and around a year later the vice chancellor of Oxford itself in 1652.[25] Yet this position of high standing was not to last for in 1658, Owen opposed the offer of the crown to Cromwell and was eventually removed from his position as vice chancellor.[26] Two years later in 1660 after the restoration of the monarchy, he left his charge of Christ Church Oxford.[27] Owen spent the remainder of his years till his death on August 24, 1683 as a dissenter who was on the outside looking into the affairs of the state, though protected by powerful noblemen.[28] Though offers would come to leave the volatile climate of England during this time (such as an offer from Harvard as well as an opportunity to pastor in Boston, Massachusetts), he felt keenly and clearly that it was his duty to stay and write with the intention of strengthening the dissenters cause and encouraging the puritan pursuit of the glory of God in the midst of great opposition.[29] He finished his days as a pastor of an independent church called Leadenhall Chapel in London, which he pastored faithfully until

20. Toon, *God's Statesman*, 1.

21. Toon, *God's Statesman*, 1.

22. Elswell, *Evangelical Dictionary of Theology*, 877.

23. Barret and Haykin, *Owen on the Christian Life*, 22.

24. Barret and Haykin, *Owen on the Christian Life*, 22.

25. Acquired this data from both Elswell. *Evangelical Dictionary of Theology*, 877, and Barret and Haykin, *Owen on the Christian*, 22.

26. Barret and Haykin, *Owen on the Christian Life*, 22.

27. Barret and Haykin, *Owen on the Christian Life*, 22.

28. Barret and Haykin, *Owen on the Christian Life*, 22.

29. Barret and Haykin, *Owen on the Christian Life*, 23.

his death in 1683. In 1689 the Act of Toleration came into effect, relieving the dissenters of their affliction at the hands of the state.[30] John Owen, till his death, was one of the strongest voices in both his preaching and in writing defending the truth and feeding the flock to endure the trials of the times.

What is evident in his writings and from the various testimonies of his life is that John Owen sought to serve Christ's church faithfully to the glory of God. Owen's mind was shaped deeply by the truths of Scripture as he seemingly strived to faithfully serve the Lord Jesus in the life of the church.[31] Now it is important always to be careful to faithfully convey with honest clarity the truth of history and thereby acknowledge that even the godliest of Christians have clay feet, meaning they have flaws. John Owen was not without his faults. He was often jealous for his reputation and did not take kindly to criticism or contradiction.[32] He also was easily irritated.[33] Yet even in these things he wanted to be more like Christ, as is evident from his writings. John Owen was an imperfect man who desired to faithfully serve the Lord Jesus in ministry and in all of life, particularly in the handling of the word of God to God's people in the local church. All of this helps us to understand the cultural context that shaped much of Owen's writing endeavors and his addressing the issue of pastoral preaching is no different. It is also helpful to see Owen's own commitment to the truth of God to understand what he wrote about pastoral preaching.

A Life Poured Out before God

Paul states in 2 Tim 4:6–8,

> For I am already being poured out as a drink offering, and the time of my departure has come. I have fought the good fight, I have finished the course, I have kept the faith; in the future there is laid up for me the crown of

30. Barret and Haykin, *Owen on the Christian Life*, 23.

31. See Thomson's *Life of John Owen* in volume 1 of Owen, *Works*.

32. Cooper, *John Owen*, 305.

33. Cooper, *John Owen*, 305.

righteousness, which the Lord, the righteous Judge, will award to me on that day; and not only to me, but also to all who have loved His appearing.[34]

Paul outlined at the end of his ministry that he had "fought the good fight," "finished the course," "kept the faith." All three of these descriptions of Paul's life and ministry convey the reality that Paul upon his conversion followed Christ fervently and faithfully and endured in doing so by God's grace to the end. The reward of such being the crown of righteousness given to the redeemed of God, who delight in the Lord's coming. What a description of Paul's life is given under the inspiration of the Holy Spirit. This description, in light of historical documentation, seems to fit John Owen's life, ministry, and commitment to the truth of Christ as well. Though he enjoyed prominence in ministry for a season in preaching to parliament, the position as Cromwell's chaplain, and eventually the position as Dean at Oxford's Christ Church for many years, that never appeared from the biographies of Owen to be his focus.[35] John Owen, whether in a village at Essex, or in a place of prominence at Oxford, or for the last twenty years of his life as a dissenter and persecuted pastor, was faithful to preach the word rightly and defend the truth clearly in his writings for the maturity in holiness of God's chosen people. Owen was a gifted and faithful Biblical scholar. Per Sinclair Ferguson, "Owen studied the strongest and best exposition of the view he opposed" to rightly understand the issues at hand and address them biblically.[36] He did not leave during the fire of governmental persecution for the privilege of a presidency at Harvard, nor did he seek to escape the difficulty of being a dissenter for the quiet life of a pastorate in Boston.[37] His life is marked by a commitment to follow Christ even in the fire

---

34. All Scriptural quotes are from NASB95 unless otherwise noted.

35. Owen never appeared to be consumed with prestige, by all accounts. Though a sinful man like us all, God in his grace preserved him unto faithfulness over enticement of influence and the acclaim of men.

36. Ferguson, *Trinitarian Devotion of John Owen*, 8.

37. Conclusion drawn from biographies by Thomson, *Life of John Owen*, in volume 1 of Owen's *Works*, and Barret and Haykin, *Owen on the Christian Life*.

of persecution from the authorities that he once preached to, and from all sorts of opposition within even his own puritan circles.[38]

From the historical evidence of John Owen's life we see the reality of a Christian committed to Christ above all. His passion was that God's people would pursue holiness in Christ as those who had been chosen by God, redeemed by Christ, and indwelled by God the Holy Spirit. John Owen saw that his life was to be salt and light to the glory of Christ. Owen knew the power of the gospel would produce fruit in his and all believers' lives. Owen wrote about holiness in his famous book *Mortification of Sin in Believers*, "By causing our hearts to abound in grace and the fruits that are contrary to the flesh, and the fruits thereof and principles of them."[39] Hearts that abound in the grace of God (the gospel) will produce the fruits (holiness) contrary to the sinful flesh of man. Owen considered it the duty of the Christian to "be perfecting holiness in the fear of God," to be "growing in grace" every day, to be "renewing our inward man day by day."[40] He believed that preachers must have experienced the power of the truth they preach.[41] He was a man whose aim was to live out the commands of Christ. As J. I. Packer stated, "his spiritual stature matched his intellectual gifts."[42] Packer went on to point out that David Clarkson in his funeral sermon for Owen defined Owen's life by the term "holiness."[43] Owen, like many of the puritans of his time, actively waged war on the inward sin nature of his own heart and desired to be conformed in all of his being to the very image of Christ. Owen in his writings highlighted truths that were both rooted in Scripture, preached those truths to those entrusted to his care, and was diligent to apply truth to his own life. He desired to be separate unto Christ as a man and a minister. It is his pastoral preaching of

38. Conclusion drawn from biographies by Thomson, *Life of John Owen*, in Owen, *Works*, and Barret and Haykin, *Owen on the Christian*.

39. Owen, *Works*, 6:19.

40. Owen, *Works*, 6:14.

41. Packer, *Quest for Godliness*, 193.

42. Packer, *Quest for Godliness*, 193.

43. Barret and Haykin, *Owen on the Christ Life*, 267.

this faithful man of the Word that we will narrow in on to analyze in light of the Holy Scriptures.

A Pastoral Heart

John Owen, though today known more for his scholarship, had a pastor's heart. He had a genuine concern for the welfare of those entrusted to his care in Christ and for the church universal. One of the greatest examples of Owen's heart for the people of God he pastored is seen in his letter to the church at Leadenhall Street, penned in 1680. In the opening of this letter a pastoral heart is on display for his congregation, whom he addressed as "Beloved in the Lord," to see as penned the following second part to his opening:

> But although I am absent from you in body, I am in mind, affection and spirit present with you, and in your assemblies; for I hope you will be found my crown and rejoicing in the day of the Lord: and my prayer for you night and day is, that you may stand fast in the whole will of God, and maintain the beginning of your confidence without wavering, firm unto the end. I know it is needless for me at this distance to write to you about what concerns you in point of duty at this season, that work being well supplied by my brother in the ministry; yet give me leave, out of my abundant affections towards you, to bring some few things to your remembrance as my weakness will permit.[44]

He went on to end the letter and sign it in the following way, "Your unworthy pastor and your servant for Jesus' sake. J. Owen."[45] John Owen, as evidenced in his letter, loved the church and his pastoral preaching clearly revolved around his life being in service to them as service unto Christ. John Owen did not just love to preach, he loved dearly those to whom he had been called to preach pastorally for the glory of his King, our Lord Jesus. The church was to be his crown and a source of rejoicing in the day of the Lord. His

---

44. Barret and Haykin, *Owen on the Christ Life*, 267.
45. Barret and Haykin, *Owen on the Christ Life*, 267.

writings on pastoral ministry, as I hope to prove, are no less than a Biblical summons to faithfully take up the charge of preaching the Word to the flock, that Christ with infinite love died for, with the greatest zeal and utmost diligence for the flock of the Lord Jesus' greatest good all to the glory of the Triune God.

Owen's Understanding of the Recipients of Pastoral Preaching—The Local Church

JOHN OWEN BELIEVED A pastor existed to serve with the word a certain group of gathered people. He wrote:

> The first and principal duty of a pastor is to feed the flock by diligent preaching of the Word. . . .This feeding is the essence of the office of pastor, as unto the exercise of it; so that he who doth not, or can to, or will not feed the flock is no pastor, whatever outward call or work he may have in the church.[1]

Owen used strong wording here to convey the imperative of preaching in the shepherding ministry of a pastor. His writing in his book *True Nature of a Gospel Church* highlighted Owen's high view of the task of preaching and its irreplaceable nature in the life of a church. In order to properly grasp the entirety of Owen's view of preaching as the essence of the office of a pastor, as well as his most important ministry, we need to understand his view of those who were to be the recipients of the preached word of God, namely the local church. John Owen's view of preaching is directly tied to his mature view of the local church.

Peter in 1 Pet 5:1–4 gives his fellow elders a strong exhortation concerning the pastoral ministry amongst the local body of believers. He states:

1. Owen, *Works*, 16:74–75.

> Therefore, I exhort the elders among you, as your fellow
> elder and witness of the sufferings of Christ, and a par-
> taker also of the glory that is to be revealed, shepherd
> the flock of God among you, exercising oversight not
> under compulsion, but voluntarily, according to the will
> of God; and not for sordid gain, but with eagerness; nor
> yet as lording it over those allotted to your charge, but
> proving to be examples to the flock. And when the Chief
> Shepherd appears, you will receive the unfading crown
> of glory.

Peter equates the role of an elder to that of a shepherd and the local church to a "flock" of sheep. The word "shepherd" here is the Greek work "*poimainō*" and is in the imperative mood, meaning this is a command for elders to perform and keep. The idea is to guide the flock, to care for the flock, to help the flock, to go before the flock, to protect the flock from those who would prey on the flock, and to feed the flock. Peter made it clear that this should be a pastor's desire and they were to do this eagerly. It is also assumed there was a group of gathered people the elder was amongst.

The very essence of the office of pastor exists for a particular people, namely the local church. John Owen seemed to echo from his quoted statements the same convictions from 1 Pet 5:1–4 and all Holy Scripture. The question that scholars have asked or implied in recent scholarship, which we will examine later in this book, of Owen's ministry revolves around whether Owen practiced what he penned. As we see from his writings, he seemed to genuinely believe that the pastoral ministry revolved around the pastor being a man of the word whose office existed for a local gathering of people who have been called out of darkness by the word of Christ in salvation. Though he operated initially in a parish system, he later advocated for the congregationalist ideology of a true regenerate church. Peter Toon writes about his assessment of Owen's mature view of the lo-cal church:

> His [Owen] doctrine of the church was based on the New
> Testament alone. He defined the church as "a society of
> persons called out of the world, or their natural worldly
> state, by the administration of the Word and Spirit, unto

obedience of the faith, or the knowledge and worship of God in Christ, joined together in a holy band, or by special agreement, for the exercise of the communion of the saints, in the due observation of all the ordinances of the gospel."[2]

Peter Toon asserted in his biographical depiction of Owen that he viewed the local church in terms of a regenerate congregation, though it could exist within a parish ministry of sorts. Before we assess Toon's claim concerning Owen's writings on the matter, let's first answer the question, briefly, on what the Scripture states concerning a local church.

What Is a Local Church?

The Greek word *ekklēsia* is the common word used in the New Testament to describe the church. It is used 114 times in the New Testament, and it carries with it the meaning of all God's people redeemed from all time in some contexts (church universal), as well as all God's people in the world or God's people in a region, and in many contexts the local gathering of God's people in a place. For example, in Eph 5:23,25 and Heb 12:23 it refers to the church invisible (universal). In Rom 16:5 as well as Col 4:15 the word is used of Spirit-indwelled people trusting in Christ alone for salvation that meets together. The church universal and local is clearly spelled out in Scripture. Now if pastoral preaching is the regular weekly proclamation of the word of God to a particular group of people, the church local, how did John Owen view the recipients of the preaching of the word in light of the Scripture? Is Toon correct in his assessment of Owen's view of the recipients of pastoral preaching? Owen in his writings expounded the truth of Holy Scripture put forth regarding the reality of what a local church is to which a pastor is to preach every Lord's Day. He stated:

In this division, let there be, in the name of Christ, and the fear of God, a gathering of professors (visible saints, men and women of good knowledge and upright

2. Toon, *God's Statesman*, 164.

conversation,—so holding forth their communion with
Christ), by their own desire and voluntary consent, into
one body,—uniting themselves, by virtue of some prom-
issory engagement or otherwise, to perform all mutual
duties, to walk in love and peace, spiritual and church
communion, as beseemth the gospel.[3]

In his book, *True Nature of a Gospel Church*, he outlined the
requirements for a person to be a member of a Biblical local church.
Owen used the following terms to define who is allotted a membership into the local church per his understanding of Scripture:

Visible, uncontrollable profession, to constitute them
subjects of Christ "kingdom," "regeneration" "of this
regeneration baptism is the symbol, the sign, the expres-
sion, and representation," "competent knowledge of the
doctrines and mystery of the gospel, especially concerning the person and offices of Christ," "professed subjec-
tion of soul and conscience unto the authority of Christ
in the church," "instruction in and consent unto the doctrine of denial and bearing of the cross," "conviction and
confession of sin, with the way of deliverance by Jesus
Christ," "the constant performance of all known duties of
religion, both of piety in the public and private worship
of God, as also of charity with respect unto others," "a
careful abstinence from all known sins," "children do be-
long unto and have interest in their parents' covenant . . .
baptizing the children of church members, giving them
thereby an admission into the visible catholic church."[4]

John Owen in this statement conveyed the importance of a
regenerate church membership that willfully submitted to Christ
in the local church and lived out the faith in public and private. He
believed that children were brought into the visible church under
their parent's covenant and were to be baptized as such. For Owen,
a person who failed to live up to the membership requirements was
to be rebuked and, if they remained unrepentant, removed from the
membership of the church.

3. Owen, *Works*, 8:51.
4. Owen, *Works*, 16:11–24.

John Owen from these statements and writings seemed to strongly believe in a congregational church government, which affirms Peter Toon's assessment mentioned earlier concerning Owen's mature thought. Owen defined the local visible church as a gathering of professors of Christ Jesus in a particular place who were covenanting with one another for accountability, growth, and fellowship in Christ.[5] Owen, in his statements, expounded that a local church was the *ekklēsia* of God in a particular area that covenanted with one another and gathered every Lord's Day around the word read, sung, preached, and prayed. Not only did he define clearly what the local church was, he applied that understanding to a variety of different contexts and scenarios. He in one sermon (not quite his mature thought as it was written earlier) suggested what the geographical boundaries should be for rural contexts whereby he advised how persons should connect with a local congregation in a rural region.[6] Thereby he showed the practical application of the doctrine of a local church (the gathering of the redeemed which he calls in this section "professors") in a region that may be more geographically spread out. He stated,

> Let the extremes of the division not be above eight or ten miles distant, and so the middle or centre not more than four or five miles any part of it,—which is no more than some usually go to preaching of the Word, and in which space Christians are generally well known to one another in the country as almost at the next door in cities; but yet this may be regulated according to the number of professors fit for the society intended,—which would not be above five hundred, nor under one hundred.[7]

The congregationalist ideology of Owen from these writings seemed to adhere to a congregationalist position that believed the church was a professing people who covenanted together in Christ. Toon's assessment appears to be an accurate summarization of

5. This statement comes from both Owen, *Works*, 8:51, and Owen, *Works*, 16:11–24.

6. Owen, *Works*, 8:50–51.

7. Owen, *Works*, 8:50–51.

Owen's view of the recipients of the pastoral preaching, the local church. More importantly Owen's view fits the narrative of what a local *ekklēsia* is per Scripture.

What Does the Local Church Gather To Do?

Why is it so imperative for the local church to gather every Lord's Day to hear the word of God preached? It seems, as Toon asserted, that Owen connected the imperative of meeting with the importance of hearing a message from God's word delivered by a man who knew the word and congregation well. John Owen believed that one of the chief responsibilities as God's people in their gatherings was to hear the word, worship the Lord, and pray fervently, as well as love one another in genuine fellowship. He wrote in his writing on the "Mutual Duties in a Church Fellowship":

> By assembling of more together, by appointment, for prayer and instruction from the word, Acts x. 24, xii. 12; Job ii.11; Eph. V.19; James v. 16; Jude 20; 1 Thess. V. 14; this being the special ordinance and appointment of God, for the increasing of knowledge, love, charity, experience, and the improving of gifts received, everyone to the building of the tabernacle.[8]

He went on to write about the overflow of the people of God gathering around the word preached which was they would also pray for the church invisible and each other in the church local. He wrote:

> Continual prayer for the prosperous state of the church, in God's protection toward it. . . . Prayer, as it is the great engine whereby to prevail with the Almighty, Isa xlv.11, so it is the sure refuge of the saints at all times, both in their own behalf, Ps. 1xi.2, and also of others, Acts xii.5.[9]

Owen in these writings perceived the local church gathering as greatly important and even quoted the great text in Acts 12 where the church gathered in Jerusalem to pray for Peter in his

8. Owen, *Works*, 13:70.
9. Owen, *Works*, 13:64.

imprisonment as a pattern to follow by God's people.[10] He understood this covenant group of people who gathered to receive the food of God's word from their local church pastor were to be a praying people unto the glory of God. As recipients of the word, he saw how in being transformed by the word they were to live out the principle of familial love before the world as a local group of people.

He also wrote about a local church being a people who genuinely cared for and loved one another. In *Mutual Duties in a Church Fellowship* he wrote:

> Love is the fountain of all duties towards God and man,
> Matt. Xxii. 37, the substance of all rules that concerneth
> the saints, the bond of communion, "the fulfilling of the
> law," Rom. xiii. 8–10, the advancement of the honour of
> the Lord Jesus, and the glory of the gospel. The primitive
> Christian had a proverbial speech, received, as they said,
> from Christ, "Never rejoice but when thou seest they
> brother in love;" and it was common among the heathens
> concerning them, "See how they love one another!"[11]

A local church, per Owen's understanding of the New Testament here, should stick out to the world because of their love for one another and their devotion to God's word as well as their fervency in prayer, all of which are true exercises of faith in Christ alone.[12] The local church as recipients of God's word delivered by the pastor was to be transformed to such a degree that they were pillars of love and piety in prayer.

How Does a Church Call a Pastor to Preach to Them?

Today there is often a lot of confusion in the Western world as to how to biblically call a pastor. Some treat it as a job opening; others as a position to be filled by some ecclesiastical authority. John Owen from his writings proposed that it was the congregation that called

10. Owen, *Works*, 13:64.

11. Owen, *Works*, 13:62.

12. Owen, *Works*, 13:62–64.

a pastor to oversee them. He placed the authority of calling a pastor to those who gathered to receive God's word as the sheep of Christ in a local area, which shows his congregationalist ideology. He had moved in his ministry to a congregational view of the church over time. Yet in his evolution of thought he stated,

> When some convenient number are thus assembled, let the ministers, if men of approved integrity and abilities, be acknowledged as elders respectively called to teach and rule in the church by virtue of their former mission, and be assumed to be so to this society by virtue of their voluntary consent and election.[13]

Per Owen the congregation as recipients of the word were to be the ones responsible for assessing and calling a pastor who had the appropriate character, understanding, and abilities to properly preach the word and care for the flock from the word of God. The church was called to recognize and elect such men to the office. This means that the recipients of pastoral preaching per Owen were the instruments that God divinely wielded to bring a man forward to preach to them week in and week out from the word.

John Owen understood that pastors were a gift from God to a local church and to function rightly had to be gifted spiritually by God to carry out the task of ministry, particularly preaching the word. Owen in one sermon stated,

> Gifts make no man a minister; but all the world cannot make a minister of Christ without gifts. If the Lord Jesus should cease to give out spiritual gifts unto men for the work of the ministry, he need do no more to take away the ministry itself; it must cease also: and it is the very way the ministry ceases in apostatizing churches—Christ no more giving out unto them of the gifts of his Spirit; and all their outward forms and order, which they can continue, are of signification in his sight.[14]

In another sermon Owen outlined that God is the one who truly makes and calls a pastor for a local church. He seemed to

13. Owen, *Works*, 8:51.

14. Owen, *Works*, 9:432.

believe that it was the local church's responsibility to recognize such a person.[15] He conveyed in a sermon this truth:

> Christ doth it by giving power unto his church to call persons to that office, by him appointed and prepared by the gifts to bestows. And you may observe three things concerning this power:
>
> 1. That this power in the church is not despotical, lordly, and absolute compliance with the command of Christ: it is but the doing what Christ hath commanded; and that gives virtue, efficacy, and power unto it. . . .
> 2. There is no power in any church to choose any one whom Christ hath not chosen before; that is, no church can make a man formally a minister, that Christ hath not made so materially, if I may so say. If Christ has not pre-instructed and prefurnished him with gifts, it is not in the power of the church to choose or call him. . . .
> 3. The way whereby the church doth call or constitute any person unto this office thus appointed, is, by giving themselves up unto him in the Lord; which they testify by their solemn choice and election by suffrage: the way, I say, is, by submitting themselves unto him in the Lord, witnessing it by their solemn suffrage in the choice of him.[16]

Pastoral preaching for Owen centered around the word of God feeding a local gathering of God's sheep, and the local covenant gathering of God's professing people, he believed here, were to call for themselves an under-shepherd who was of the biblically required character and capability to do so. He understood that the greatest need any gathering of God's people had was to hear from God's word rightly for that was hearing from God. If hearing the word rightly was removed from the local church, then that local church would likely drift away from truth and into apostasy over

---

15. Owen, *Works*, 9:432.
16. Owen, *Works*, 9:433.

time.[17] John Owen saw the pastoral task as an immense one. He understood that the under-shepherding oversight of the flock had significant ramifications for the flocks well-being and growth. He wrote:

> Let the ministers engage themselves in a special manner to watch over his flock, every one according to his abilities, both in teaching, exhorting, and ruling, so often as occasion shall be administered, for things that contain ecclesiastical rule and church order; acting jointly and as in a classical combination, and putting forth all authority that such cases are intrusted with.[18]

Pastoral preaching was the top priority for John Owen in pastoral ministry because the flock of God was precious to Christ Jesus the King of glory. The recipients of pastoral preaching were also the instrument in the hand of God to assess and call a man to preach to them from the word. They were a gathering of Christians who had the responsibility to call to themselves one who would feed them well the word. It is clear from Owen's writings on the local church and how they called a pastor that he adhered to congregationalist view in his maturing and mature thought, which seems to best fit the Scriptural example as highlighted at the beginning of this chapter. In light of Owen's understanding of the recipients of pastoral preaching and their authority it naturally follows to examine the aim of the gathering of those who were the recipients of pastoral preaching to further study his view of a local church.

The Aim of the Local Church's Gathering

Why meet as a local group of Christians? Often we do not see the aim of such gatherings. John Owen wrote on the aim of the church thereby implying the aim of the local gathering in volume 13 of his *Works*. He wrote:

17. Owen, *Works*, 9:51432.
18. Owen, *Works*, 8:51.

> Holiness becometh the house of the Lord for ever; with-
> out it none shall see God. Christ died to wash his church,
> to present it before his Father without spot or blemish;
> to purchase unto himself a peculiar people, zealous for
> good works. It is the kingdom of God within us, and
> by which it appeared unto all that we are children of
> the kingdom. Let this, then, be the great discriminating
> character of the church from the world, that they are
> holy, humbled, self-denying people. Our Master is holy;
> his doctrine and worship are holy; Let us strive that our
> hearts may also be holy.[19]

The local church was to be growing, as it gathered in loving
unity around the word and prayer, in holiness in order to reflect
increasingly the glory of God to the watching world.[20] The recipients of pastoral preaching, the local church, gathered to worship
God and be transformed by the word of God. The weekly gathering
under the word preached was to produce holiness in the hearts of
the redeemed of Christ per John Owen's understanding. Scripture
attests to this purpose (1 Pet 1:14–16) for the gathering of God's
people in Scripture. For example, in Heb 10:24–25 the author of
Hebrews exhorts his hearers to not forsake the gathering together
in order to exhort one another on in love and good deeds, which are
essential aspects of lives lived unto the glory of God. This is what
Owen strived for in his pastoral preaching. He understood that one
of the greatest ordinary means of grace God has given his people
to grow in humility and holiness to the praise of God's name is the
pastoral preaching of the word each week. He wrote, "A man is pastor unto them whom he feeds by pastoral teaching, and to more."[21]
John Owen saw the means of the word of God preached weekly to
the church as one of the greatest ways God had ordained to achieve
the aim of holiness in his redeemed people who gather each Lord's
Day. The recipients of pastoral preaching from Owen's view was
clearly those who have been saved out of the world, meet weekly
together around the word, were responsible for calling a man to

19. Owen, *Works*, 13:64.

20. Owen, *Works*, 13:64.

21. Owen, *Works*, 16:75.

preach to them pastorally, all with the aim of growing into Christ-like holiness. From his statements on holiness and the pastor's role of preaching, that seems to be the best conclusion concerning his thought on the gathering of God's people under the word preached. Per Owen, local churches were a congregation of believers around the word preached unto the end that they are conformed to the holy character of Christ Jesus and thereby give God much glory in how they stand apart from the unholy mass of humanity. Having covered Owen's view of the recipients of pastoral preaching, it is clear he held a congregational view, which seems to best fit the New Testament perspective of the local church, the recipients of pastoral preaching. It is necessary to next examine, in greater detail, the priority of pastoral preaching per John Owen's writings to further assess Owen's understanding of pastoral preaching considering Holy Scripture.

Owen's Understanding of the Priority of Pastoral Preaching

WHAT IS TO BE a pastor's priority in pastoral ministry? Paul exhorts Timothy, as he awaits his sentence of death:

> I solemnly charge you in the presence of God and of Christ Jesus, who is to judge the living and the dead, and by His appearing and His kingdom: preach the word; be ready in season and out of season; reprove, rebuke, exhort, with great patience and instruction. For the time will come when they will not endure sound doctrine; but wanting to have their ears tickled, they will accumulate for themselves teachers in accordance to their own desires, and will turn away their ears from the truth and will turn aside to myths. But you, be sober in all things, endure hardship, do the work of an evangelist, fulfill your ministry.[1]

Paul's greatest concern in his parting words with his son in the faith, a pastor and elder, was that Timothy would be found faithful in all seasons to be preaching the word of God. That the people of God would be fed the truth of God rightly from Timothy's clear and precise exposition of the Scripture. Why was this so important to Paul? The answer to that question is found in what Paul had said right before 2 Tim 4:1–5. In 2 Tim 3:16–17 Paul the apostle stated:

> All Scripture is inspired by God and profitable for teaching, for reproof, for correction, for training in

---

1. 2 Tim 4:1–5.

righteousness; so that the man of God may be adequate, equipped for every good work."

Paul taught that the word of God alone gave the people of God the right knowledge of God, convicted them of their sin, called them to righteous living, and equipped them for every good work. The word of God per Paul was inspired by God. Did John Owen emphasize what we see Paul emphasize here with regards to the pastoral ministry of a man called to serve a local church?

Some modern scholarship would not necessarily answer yes to that question. Owen has been accused of addressing even in his sermons to the Leadenhall church a multitude of politically charged messages that stemmed from a faulty apocalyptic worldview. Crawford Gribben, in his book *John Owen and English Puritanism*, wrote, "For Owen would preach to his small congregation messages that he could not dare commit to print, messages that experimented with prognostication and the sometimes politically charged interpretation of providence."[2] Kelly Kapic wrote concerning Owen's preaching in his role as a statesman:

> Employing the "Israelite paradigm," Owen took on a prophetic role in warning the nation and especially the leaders of the government. He made no simple equation between England and Israel, but the way Israel functioned served as a type or pattern to understand how God might be relating to England in his day. Similarly, Owen looked to the Old Testament stories, filled with assurances and threats, as the way in which to make sense of the current experiences of England.[3]

Kelly Kapic's statement concerning Owen's preaching is focused on his speaking to parliament and other officials as a statesman who saw the imperative for England to promote the reformed faith as a nation. Martyn Cowan wrote, referencing Owen's sermon *Faith's Answer to Divine Reproofs*:

---

2. Gribben, *John Owen and English Puritanism*, 239.
3. Kapic, "John Owen and the Civil War Apocalypse," 905.

> Owen described how the "public minister of the church" may be spoken of "as a prophet" whose task was to explain God's "special design" towards the church in the "calamities" and "devastation" brought upon church and nation.[4]

While no one would seem to deny Kapic and Cowan's conclusions concerning Owen's ministry as a statesman this does not necessarily prove that Owen took such prophetic preaching into the pulpit of his local church in his later years consistently. The idea examined by Cowan and Gribben is that a lot of political proclamation was incorporated in Owen's sermons to the flock that gathered as two combined churches at Leadenhall. While it may genuinely be the case that his political views occasionally made its way into some of his sermons in an unhelpful manner, it does not prove that political providential ideology was Owen's focus as a local church pastor. This proposal seems difficult to prove for we only have a few sermons that others transcribed, or he published which does not necessarily provide the evidence for such a claim that he was more concerned about being a political prophet than the salvation and growth in personal holiness of those entrusted to his care in his endeavors as a local church pastor. Gribben implicitly acknowledges this weakness in his statement that most of Owen's sermons were not put to print.

Peter Toon, an early twentieth-century biographer of John Owen would not necessarily agree with Crawford Gribben and Martyn Cowan's perspective. Peter Toon, in his book *God's Statesman*, wrote:

> Only a small proportion of the many sermons that Owen preached to the Congregational church in Leadenhall Street between 1673 and 1683 were ever printed. From these it is clear that he regarded his principal task as a preacher to be that of carefully expounding and explaining the nature of the biblical view of the Christian life and witness, exhorting his hearers zealously to obey and seek after God and to cultivate the grace of God in their hearts. He placed great stress not only upon sound

4. Cowan, *John Owen and the Civil War Apocalypse*, 183.

doctrine but also upon actual experience of God in Christian worship and in the soul of believers."[5]

In line with Peter Toon's view John Owen, from his writings, did not see pastoral preaching as a platform primarily to express political ideals based in apocalyptic ideology. Owen wrote in *True Nature of a Gospel Church*:

> The first and principal duty of a pastor is to feed the flock by diligent preaching of the Word. . . . *This feeding is the essence of the office of pastor*, as unto the exercise of it; so that he who doth not, or can to, or will not feed the flock is no pastor, whatever outward call or work he may have in the church.[6]

The access we do have to printed sermons during his time primarily as a pastor, not the sermons he preached while in the position of University Provost or National Statesman, do not seem to support the proposition of Cowan and others that Owen was often driven in his messages by an apocalyptic worldview with England at the center. For example, Owen's sermon "Gospel Charity" from Colossians 3:14 is clearly an exposition of the passage applied to Owen's church joining with Leadenhall to become one fellowship. Owen stated in this sermon:

> I thought to have given you many other directions; but I must conclude. If God be pleased to imprint any thing from this word upon our hearts and spirits, we shall have cause to rejoice in it. However, remember thus much, that you were begged and entreated,—as you regard the glory of God, the honour of the gospel, and the edification of this church (which of two is now become one), concerning which you must all in your places give an account, as well as I in mine, and as you have any respect unto the ministry of him whom God hath set over you,—that all be wound up in this one duty of love; which if God please

---

5. Toon, *God's Statesman*, 157–58.
6. Owen, *Works*, 16:74–75. Emphasis mine.

to increase, and make intense among us, I no way doubt but he will prosper this day's work of our union.[7]

Owen's pastoral concern that his preaching would rightly apply the Holy Scripture to the local gathering of God's people is powerfully seen in this sample. Yet while it may be far from solidifying the point that Owen's preaching to the congregational church he pastored for the last two decades of his life was consistently pastoral in nature, not habitually political in content, it does provide support to Toon's assertion. It is no accident that John Owen emphatically called pastors of his time to feed the flock of Christ the word for their maturity in the faith. John Owen, from his writings, believed pastoral preaching to a local church to be the main calling of a pastor. I hope to prove that Owen put forth a clear priority for preaching in the ministry of a pastor, in his writings, that was rooted in his high view of Scripture such as 2 Tim 3:16–4:5. He understood that the main and primary job of a pastor is to feed the flock the word of God correctly explained for the glory of God. Toon believed Owen to be a man who prioritized Biblical preaching to the local church for their understanding of truth and therein experiencing the one true God in salvation and joyful sanctification.

In order to show that Owen shared Paul's view of the word's importance for the church as seen in 2 Tim 3:16 as well as Paul's emphasis for the pastor to preach the word, I will discuss Owen's writings in the four following subcategories: first, his view of the word of God; second, his view of preaching as the primary ministry of the pastor; third, the importance of the preacher practicing what he preaches to solidify the message; lastly, Owen's clear belief that if one cannot preach, then he should not be a pastor.

The Word of God

A high view of the Bible will bring a high esteem of faithful preaching. Why did Owen prioritize biblically faithful preaching? Per his own writings he valued the Scriptures as God's word. Therefore, it naturally followed that preaching the word was an ordinary means

7. Owen, *Works*, 9:271.

of grace God ordained to impart spiritual life into the spiritually dead hearts of people and grow believers into maturity in Christ. Wayne Grudem would define the proclamation of the word in these helpful terms before we examine Owen's view:

> Even before people become Christians, The Word of God as preached and taught brings God's grace to them in that it is the instrument God uses to impart spiritual life to them and bring them to salvation. . . . Moreover, once we become Christians, Paul reminds us that it is the Word of God that "is able to build you up" (Acts 20:32). It is necessary for spiritual nourishment and for maintaining spiritual life, because we do not live on bread alone but on "every word that proceeds from the mouth of God" (Matt. 4:4).[8]

Like theologians after and before, Owen's view of preaching as a means of grace to God's people centered on the belief that the Scriptures were infallible and sufficient. The reason Owen was so ardent about the priority of the right preaching of God's word was that he understood that it was the word of God that revealed God to the mind/inner life of a person, convicted of sin, called sinners to faith, and grew the redeemed in the faith. He also knew that the pastor's authority in the congregation was only based on his faithful preaching of and servant leadership in the word of God, for the word of God is the authority over the church.

John Owen's high view of preaching cannot be divorced from his immense love of the Scripture and his belief in the sufficiency of the Scripture. He wrote in *The Divine Original of Scripture*:

> Now as the Scripture is thus a light, we grant it to be the duty of the church, of any church, of every church, to hold it up, whereby it may become the more conspicuous. It is a pillar and ground to set this light upon. . . . And this duty it performs ministerially, not authoritatively. A church may bear up the light-it is not the light. . . . All the preaching that is in any church, its administration of ordinances, all its walking in the truth, hold up this light.[9]

8. Grudem, *Systematic Theology*, 952.
9. Owen, *Works*, 16:320–21.

Owen compared the Scripture to light and what he means is it conveyed "the majesty of its Author," "illuminating" truth and conveying righteousness.[10] John Owen put forth clearly that the word of God is God's revelation of God to man.[11] Owen understood that the word is the source of understanding the great truths of God, such as the persons of the One Triune God, his commands, his offer of salvation, and his attributes seen in his redemptive as well as punitive works throughout the historical narrative of the Scriptures. The Scripture per Owen is light to our darkness. Most know the feeling of walking into a dark room, unsure of what is on the floor or on the walls or what may be in the room. However, when the light switch is flipped, the room and its contents are illuminated, just as when the word of God is preached the light switch of God's glory is flipped, illuminating to the human heart the truth of God. The word of God illuminates the holiness of God and the black room of man's depraved soul so that it may see its unholiness and need for the Savior, the Lord Jesus. Owen's thought was that the word of God, per his own statement, is that which brings God's truth to the minds and affections of fallen man to make them new inwardly. The word was the light of God to be shined into the heart of every man and woman that came into the assembly on any Lord's Day. The preaching of the word was to "hold up this light" so that men and women may come into contact with the Holy God and find hope in the saving work of the Lion of the tribe of Judah, who is the Lamb that was slain.[12] This emphasis from Owen seems to show that he did not view the pulpit as primarily a place for political statements; though, when the Scripture allowed, he likely would address national affairs. If the word reveals God, then is it any wonder why John Owen demanded it be the highest priority of any true pastor, who is commanded in Scripture to convey the truth of God to the people of God?[13]

10. Owen, *Works*, 16:320.

11. Owen, *Works*, 16:321.

12. Owen, *Works*, 16:320–21.

13. Owen, *Works*, 16:74–75.

Preaching as the Primary Ministry of a Pastor

Charles II once asked John Owen why anyone would listen to the preaching ministry of a fellow dissenting pastor in his time that was a tinker who lacked formal education, a preacher named John Bunyan.[14] John Owen is quoted as replying, "Could I possess the tinker's abilities for preaching, please your majesty, I would gladly relinquish all my learning."[15] It is clear from statements such as these that Owen viewed preaching as primarily something that benefited the flock of the Lord Jesus not fueled by apocalyptic ideologies applied to his time as he has been accused of by scholars such as Gribben. John Owen saw preaching as the primary ministry of a pastoral ministry per the Biblical commands found in Holy Scripture (John 21:15–25; Acts 20:17–31; Eph 4:11–15; 2 Tim 4:1–2).[16] Barret and Haykin state in their book on John Owen:

> John Owen is widely regarded as one of the most influential English Puritans. As a pastor, he longed to see the glory of Christ take root in people's lives. As a writer, he continues to encourage us toward discipline and communion with God.[17]

Their analysis of Owen seems to prove true from his own writings, especially his priority of preaching being that God's people may grow in their affections for the Lord Jesus. Owen stated in *The True Nature of a Gospel Church* the following:

> The first and principal duty of a pastor is to feed the flock by diligent preaching of the Word. It is a promise relating to the New Testament that God would give unto his church "pastors according to his own heart, which should feed them with knowledge and understanding," Jer. iii.15. This is by teaching or preaching the Word, and no otherwise. This feeding is the essence of the office of pastor, as unto the exercise of it; so that he who doth not,

14. Barret and Haykin, *Owen on the Christian Life*, 23.

15. Barret and Haykin, *Owen on the Christian Life*, 23.

16. Owen, *Works*, 16:74–75.

17. Barrett, "Who Is John Owen?," 12.

or can to, or will not feed the flock is no pastor, whatever outward call or work he may have in the church.[18]

This statement is packed to the brim with a summation of Owen's ideology when it comes to the preaching of the word of God. Notice what John Owen says in the opening of this statement concerning what preaching is. He defines pastoral preaching as simply "feeding the flock of God from the Word of God."[19] He clearly outlined the primary duty of a preaching pastor/elder is to feed the flock. The flock is pictured in need of food to sustain them in their existence. The food for sustenance of the spiritual person per Owen was the word preached. Owen in his book *The True Nature of a Gospel Church* stated the following, "The care of preaching the gospel was committed to Peter, and in in him unto all true pastors of the church, under the name of "feeding, 'John xxi. 15–17."[20] For a flock to be properly nourished and thereby to function as designed they are to be fed nutritiously by the pastor from the proper interpretation, proclamation, and application of the Scripture.[21]

Owen made it clear that what was at stake with regards to the preaching ministry of a pastor is the very spiritual health of the flock of God. By using such language, he meant precisely what he had stated. If the flock is not be well-fed, then logically, they would be malnourished at best and starved at worst. If fed inappropriate portions and non-nutritious sermons, they would not function as designed, just as a malnourished physical body would not function as designed by God. Owen conveyed on the forefront the grave importance of proper pastoral preaching. He stated about preaching, "this feeding is the essence of the office of pastor."[22] By using the word "essence," which means the nature of something or the most significant part of something, Owen seemingly made a very strong case and point for pastoral preaching in the life of a pastor. The very nature and most significant part of the pastor's office

18. Owen, *Works*, 16:74–75.
19. Owen, *Works*, 16:74–75.
20. Owen, *Works*, 16:75.
21. Owen, *Works*, 16:75.
22. Owen, *Works*, 16:74–75.

per Owen was the proper preaching of the word so that the flock of Christ may be sustained and grown spiritually. As a proper diet helps a growing child become an adult, so a proper diet of the word in the local church helps a babe in Christ become a mature follower in Christ. He could not express that reality with more clear terms. Clearly Owen's writing matched the teaching of Paul's exhortation to Timothy in 2 Tim 4:1–2 with regards to pastoral preaching.

Truth of the Preached Word Seen in the Pastor's Life

He practices what he preaches. This phrase is held to ministers' lives with regards to their conduct in the life of their family, the church family, and the community. Paul tells Timothy in 1 Timothy 4:16, "Pay close attention to yourself and to your teaching; persevere in these things, for as you do this you will ensure salvation both for yourself and for those who hear you." The idea is that Timothy is to keep faithful to apostolic doctrine and his life is to match the apostolic doctrine he holds to. For the Biblical narrative preaching is the priority for pastoral ministry as seen in 2 Tim 4:1–2 and a testimony of the truth pastors preach must be seen in their own life. John Owen would have agreed with this sentiment wholly. Owen believed the truth of Scripture must be a reality evident in the pastor's own life for him to be faithful in ministry and life. If preaching was truly the pastor's priority, his message must be seen in his everyday life increasingly. Owen wrote in *Eshcol, A Cluster of the Fruit of Canaan: Mutual Duties of a Church Fellowship*, "If a man teach uprightly and walk crookedly, more will fall down in the night of his life than he built in the day of his doctrine."[23] He goes on in the same book to state:

> Now, as to the completing of the exemplary life of a minister, it is required that the principle of it be that of the life of Christ in him, Gal. ii. 20, that when he hath taught others he be not himself "a cast away."[24]

23. Owen, *Works*, 13:57.
24. Owen, *Works*, 13:57.

John Owen from comments such as this as well as his demands for Christians to pursue holiness in his book, *The Mortification of Sin*, would likely have had great difficulty with the state of modern ministry in the Western world today.

Owen emphasized that "able to teach" (gifting) is only listed as one of many qualifications for eldership and the preaching ministry of the Word. Remember Owen wrote, "If a man teach uprightly and walk crookedly, more will fall down in the night of his life than he built in the day of his doctrine."[25] For Owen, gifting was not enough. A man had to practice what he preached rightly from the Word of God. As Paul tells Titus in Titus 1:15–16:

> To the pure, all things are pure; but to those who are defiled and unbelieving, nothing is pure, but both their mind and their conscience are defiled. They profess to know God, but by their deeds they deny Him, being detestable and disobedient and worthless for any good deed.

A pastor must know God and walk with him in order to be qualified to proclaim him to his redeemed people.

However, that is not to say that gifting did not matter in light of the high priority of preaching. It matters greatly per 1 Tim 3:1–5 and Titus 1. Owen emphasized this reality for the preacher. Owen highlighted the priority of a pastor's character for the pastor to be considered and called to preach the word. However, it would be a mistake to think he stopped just at character. He emphasized character but also combined it with competence to preach in order for a man to fill a pulpit rightly.

Cannot Preach Then Not a Pastor

A lot of times people can drift from one extreme to the next. It is always helpful to avoid such tendencies. To say the character of the person who is seeking the office of elder matters is not to say that

---

25. Owen, *Works*, 13:57.

gifting does not matter. Gifting matters greatly as well to the glory of God! Paul in Romans 12:6–8 writes:

> Since we have gifts that differ according to the grace given to us, each of us is to exercise them accordingly: if prophecy, according to the proportion of his faith; if service, in his serving; or he who teaches, in his teaching; or he who exhorts, in his exhortation; he who gives, with liberality; he who leads, with diligence; he who shows mercy, with cheerfulness.

The concept Paul puts forth is that every Christian is gifted by God the Holy Spirit with abilities that are to be used for the good of the church of the Lord Jesus. Genuinely called ministers of God are therefore gifted by God for the work of feeding the flock of God. They are "able to teach" as Paul writes to Timothy about elders in 1 Tim 3:2.

John Owen's view of pastoral preaching, though rooted in godly character, went beyond just character qualifications to evaluating whether a man had been gifted of God for such a vital work. Paul's admonition to Timothy about elders being able to teach seems to have stuck with Owen in his assessment of pastoral candidates. As mentioned earlier Owen's wrote, "Gifts make no man a minister; but all the world cannot make a minister of Christ without gifts."[26] He demanded that pastors be able to preach if they were truly to be a pastor.[27] It was unthinkable to Owen for a man to be confirmed to a pastorate if he could not correctly expound the Scriptures every Lord's Day just as it would have been for Paul per 1 Tim 3:2 with "able to teach." He stated, "this feeding is the essence of the office of pastor, as unto the exercise of it; so that *he who doth not, or can to, or will not feed the flock is no pastor,* whatever outward call or work he may have in the church."[28] For Owen, in this statement a man must be able to teach the Bible and proclaim it correctly to fill

---

26. Owen, *Works,* 9:432.

27. Owen, *Works,* 16:75.

28. Owen, *Works,* 16:75. Emphasis mine. Owen viewed ability to teach the Bible as vital for ministry of a pastor to such a degree that if one would not, could not properly explain/proclaim the Scriptures they were not a pastor.

the office of a pastor, no exceptions allowed. If a pastor did not have the proper tool kit, the God-given ability, and the understanding of Scripture to rightly interpret, expound, and thereby proclaim the Scripture, then that person was not a true pastor no matter what a church had externally confirmed with regards to that man. The argument is something like this: a fisherman who cannot fish should not be a fisherman, an accountant who cannot count should not be an accountant, a doctor who does not know anatomy and medicine should not practice, and a pastor who knows not the word well and cannot preach should not take a pulpit and hold the office of pastor. Every office has a function and if a person does not have the gifts to fulfill the function, they should not hold the office. The preaching elder/pastor had to be able to correctly explain the Scriptures and thereby feed the flock, for that was their function to do so in the local church. John Owen expounds further concerning the capability of a true preacher and their preaching ministry in order to protect churches from error:

"(1) A clear, sound, comprehensive knowledge of the entire doctrine of the gospel. (2) Love of the truth which they have so learned and comprehended. (3) A conscious care and fear of giving countenance and encouragement unto novel opinions. (4) Learning and ability of mind to discern and disprove the oppositions of the adversaries of the truth. (5) The solid comprehension of the most important truths of the gospel. (6) A diligent watch over their own flocks against the craft of seducers from without, or the springing up of any bitter root of error among themselves. (7) A concurrent assistance with the elders and messengers of other churches with whom they are in communion, in the declaration of the faith they all profess."[29]

Owen, like Paul in 1 Tim 3:2, called for and even demanded that anyone who would climb into a pulpit had to be able to proclaim the word of God faithfully to a congregation on the Lord's Day, as well on any occasion. Paul in Titus 1:9 takes the ideology of ability to teach (defend and expound sound doctrine) and adds reasoning behind it with regards to the high priority of preaching.

29. Owen, *Works*, 16:82–83.

Paul states in Titus 1:9, "He must hold firm to the trustworthy word as taught, so that he may be able to give instruction in sound doctrine and also to rebuke those who contradict it." Like Paul to Titus, Owen believed a pastor must be a man who had to have a sound understanding of the doctrine of the gospel, love of the truth, appropriate learning, an awareness of what is threatening the flock, and a fellowship with like-minded pastors for mutual accountability in the calling therein (which is not something Paul had said directly but could be implied from unity texts such as Christ's high priestly prayer in John 17:20–21).[30] A pastor who did not fit this criterion was one who would not be able to rightly defend the doctrines of the faith nor be able to approach the Scripture in a way that would ultimately be a benefit and help to a local gathering of God's people.[31] Therefore, such a person was not qualified for the office of pastor per Paul's writing and per John Owen's understanding all of Scripture. Owen would have seen putting pastors in pulpits who are unable to preach the word with accuracy as a grave error because of his high emphasis on the priority of preaching. In the time of the author, in many denominations what is required of a person is that they will be willing, "feel called," eager, and a relatively moving speaker. John Owen from his writings would likely strongly urge caution. The feeding of the flock the word of God was such a priority to Owen that a person who endeavored to do so must be equipped to teach the Bible correctly and accurately before he should ever enter into a pulpit to preach to the precious people of God. Owen's thinking from his writings fit the ideology we see in Paul's writings in 1 and 2 Timothy as well as Titus.

It is helpful to also remember that Owen was at one time the Dean of Christ Church Oxford and Vice Chancellor. He had a vested interest in the equipping of young men for the ministry because of the priority of preaching. I once heard a seminary professor describe the lifelong lesson he learned from a seminary president.[32]

30. Owen, *Works*, 16:82–83.

31. Owen, *Works*, 16:82–83.

32. This is a story shared by a professor concerning his interaction with the President of Southeastern Baptist Theological Seminary's at the time of his matriculation. I'm unable to find the exact message this story was shared, but

He had made the remark to the seminary president that he did not need all this learning. He should be out preaching now without having to sit in class and wait for his time to go out into the world. The seminary president had this man carry a bucket of sand with him wherever he went. The president of this seminary reminded the young man that the apostle Paul spent approximately two and a half years in Arabia preparing for the ministry Christ Jesus had called him to. If Paul needed time in the word so too did he and all students who would proclaim the word of God. The sand was to remind this student of Paul's time in Arabia and thereby the importance of having the tools to properly teach the Holy Scripture. John Owen, per his statements, would likely have greatly agreed with the president of the seminary because of his view of the priority of faithful pastoral preaching in the local church. A pastor must be able to preach the word with accuracy and clarity by God's grace. A pastor is to have the tool kit and ability to carry out this charge and task. Just as a physician must be medically trained and a lawyer versed in the fine points of the law, so too a pastor who preaches to a flock must be trained well in the Holy Scriptures and doctrine therein. What is at stake is nothing less than the souls of those in the congregation per Paul the apostle and John Owen many years after him.

A Moral Duty

Preaching, to John Owen, was not just the primary function of a pastor and therefore the highest of the pastor's priorities. For Owen, it was a moral duty of the highest importance to be undertaken with the most reverence possible of one truly called of God into the pastoral office. Owen wrote that the duty of a pastor is to "declare the gospel, when called by the providence of God thereunto, for the work of preaching unto the conversion of souls *being a moral duty*."[33] He believed resolutely that preaching was a *moral duty* of a pastor, particularly with the unconverted in mind. He understood

---

this synopsis covers what the professor conveyed.

33. Owen, *Works*, 13:56. Emphasis mine.

well that the gospel would build the sheep and call the lost sheep into the fold. Preaching for Owen thus was not only a holy charge, but an issue of great moral importance that must be adhered to with the greatest dedication. He saw the word of God as something that gave the ordinances (the Lord's Supper and Baptism) their authority and the word was entrusted to the shepherds of Christ's flock. He stated in a sermon:

> The administration of the seals of the covenant is committed unto them, as stewards of the house of Christ; for unto them the authoritative dispensation of the word is committed, whereunto the administration of the seals is annexed; for their principal end is the peculiar confirmation and application of the Word preached.[34]

Owen, in his book *True Nature of a Gospel Church*, emphasized the word of God has been entrusted to pastors as a holy and sacred stewardship.[35] Again, per Owen it was a serious stewardship that was a moral imperative to perform faithfully.[36]

Was Owen's view in accordance with what Scripture conveys concerning the role of a pastor being a steward of the truth? The story of Joseph the son of Jacob in Genesis highlights the idea of faithful stewardship well. In Gen 39, Joseph, as a steward, managed the assets and affairs of his master, Potiphar. Joseph's story highlights that a steward is one who manages the assets of their master. In Matt 25:14–30, Jesus expounds the truth of Biblical stewardship through the parable of the talents whereby a master entrusted several men with a sum of talents and they were to multiply what was given to them while their master was away. Faithfulness to steward what was given them was the criteria of evaluation upon the master's return. For the talents belonged to the master. Two of the three servants mentioned in Christ's parable heard the same affirmation, "Well done, my good and faithful servant." The servant who did nothing with what the master had entrusted to him was cast away into darkness and destruction. The point was how the servants

34. Owen, *True Nature of a Gospel Church*, 79.

35. Owen, *True Nature of a Gospel Church*, 79.

36. Owen, *Works*, 13:56.

handled what had been entrusted to them and showed their love (or lack thereof for the third servant) for their master. John Owen put forth that pastoral ministry, particularly pastoral preaching, is a stewardship by which men were entrusted with the word of God to feed the flock of Christ Jesus. Therefore, it was a moral obligation that could not be neglected for true pastors.

Paul states in 1 Cor 9:16 a similar sentiment. Paul states in 1 Cor 9:16, "For if I preach the gospel, that gives me no ground for boasting. For necessity is laid upon me. Woe to me if I do not preach the gospel!" Paul connected the priority of preaching the Gospel with its necessity for a man called by God. To not do so was to be morally in error before God. Paul said "woe" to him if he did not preach. Paul in Col 1:25 calls his ministry a stewardship from God which in Col 1:29 he labored at per God's grace in him. Owen's perspective of pastoral stewardship seemingly is rooted in the same ideology that we find in Pauline literature as well as the Scriptural narrative of stewardship. It was a moral duty. Owen held that pastors as stewards are to be found faithful before the Lord Jesus, the Master of the church. Like Paul, Owen saw faithful pastoral preaching for the pastor of a flock to be a moral imperative.

Owen's Understanding
of Pastoral Preaching

JESUS WAS MOMENTS AWAY from his betrayal and hours away from his crucifixion. After exhorting his disciples with truths about his kingdom and the coming Helper, he prayed his high priestly prayer. As part of that prayer the Lord Jesus makes a profound statement. He states in his high priestly prayer, "Sanctify them in the truth; Your word is truth."[1] He asks that God the Father would set apart his disciples by the truth, which he defined as the word of God. The implications of this statement are profound. The word of God, the Lord Jesus put forth, is the means that God had ordained to set apart his people in their conformance to Christ's character. Jesus' main priority in ministry was preaching. Of all the things God the Father could have chosen for his sinless Son to spend his days doing and being, God sent his Son to primarily be a preacher of the word. Jesus said to those seeking him for various things in Luke 4:43–44: "I must preach the kingdom of God to the other cities also, for I was sent for this purpose." Luke, the author of that Gospel account, follows that verse up with this next statement: "So He kept on preaching in the synagogues of Judea.

The Lord Jesus was sent by the Father to preach. Why is this? Preaching of the truth of the kingdom of God from the Holy Scriptures is the means God had ordained to bring out of darkness all those whom he had chosen. The word of God being expounded correctly is God's chosen means for Christ Jesus to claim the reward

1. John 17:17.

of his suffering. The truth encased in Scripture is what changes people and brings them to God. In the section following, I will dissect how John Owen viewed sermon preparation, preaching, as well as understood the importance of preaching the word faithfully by the gracious power of the Holy Spirit in light of the Biblical theology around pastoral preaching to determine if Owen's views were rightly rooted in Scripture. To rightly study Owen's view of such things it is helpful to first define what preaching is exactly per Scripture and how preachers biblically are told to approach the preaching event.

What Is Faithful Pastoral Preaching?

Paul in 2 Tim 2:15 expects his young mentee (a pastor) and thereby all heralds of the word to handle the word rightly. He states in 2 Tim 2:15, "Be diligent to present yourself approved to God as a workman who does not need to be ashamed, accurately handling the word of truth." Timothy as a pastor was to "handle" the word of God appropriately, meaning he was to rightly explain, teach, and expound the Scriptures. Timothy was to herald the truths of Scripture on behalf of King Jesus to the people redeemed by the Lord Jesus. Pastoral preaching is thus the public exposition of Scripture by those whom Christ has commissioned, equipped, and called to herald his Scripture to a local congregation. Martyn Lloyd Jones in his book *Preaching and Preachers* states this about true pastoral preaching rooted in the truth of 2 Tim 2:15:

> Any true definition of preaching must say that man is there to deliver the message of God, a message from God to those people. If you prefer the language of Paul, he is "an ambassador for Christ." That is what he is. He has been sent, he is a commissioned person, and he is standing there as the mouthpieces of God and of Christ to address these people. . . . Preaching, in other words, is a transaction between the preacher and the listener. It does something for the soul of man, for the whole of the person, the entire man; it deals with him in a vital and radical manner.[2]

2. Jones, *Preaching and Preachers*, 53.

Preaching per Lloyd Jones understanding of the Holy Scriptures was the proclamation of a message (the Bible rightly explained) to a people (those who came together under the banner of King Jesus). From all this data a working definition of Biblical expository preaching can be summarized as the following: faithful expository preaching is simply reading a text, explaining and expounding the text in light of its grammatical historical context, and applying the truth of the text, all with faithfulness and fire to God's people. Did John Owen view preaching as this? In the following section I hope to prove that John Owen in his preaching of the word would seem to have heartily affirmed the definition from the Scripture of preaching presented above and summarized in Lloyd Jones's statement on preaching. We have already examined how for John Owen the preaching ministry of a pastor centered around the faithful exposition of the Bible to a local gathering of God's people.[3] We have already seen how he defined the recipients of pastoral preaching (local church) who meet around the word of God rightly expounded. Owen demanded in his writings that pastors are to give themselves to the diligent study of Scripture to feed the flock of Christ, purchased by Christ's own blood. He demanded that pastor's study with great fervency to explain, proclaim and apply the Holy Scriptures to the flock of Christ that God had entrusted to their care.

Analysis of Owen's View of Pastoral Preaching in Light of Scripture

Owen viewed the pastors preaching as having authority only when the Word was being expounded properly and practiced. He stated:

> The Word and all ordinances dispensed in the administration to him (the pastor) committed, by virtue of ministerial authority, *are to be diligently attended and submitted unto*, with ready obedience in the Lord.[4]

3. Owen, *Works*, 8:509.
4. Owen, *Works*, 13:59. Emphasis mine.

The pastor was to preach the word for it was his office to do so. The truth of the word of God was authoritative over the flock of Christ and must be adhered to. The word of God is what built the church of God. Therefore, per Owen the pastor was to teach and herald the truth of the word of God for the joyful submission of the flock of Christ unto Christ's commands and Lordship.

John Owen clearly in his statements highlighted above understood the authority in preaching was solely based in the pastor's faithfulness to the word of God. For Owen Scripture was what created God's people. He stated,

> The Scripture hath its authority, in relation to us, before the church pass its judgment concerning it; and therefore hath not that authority from the church. . . . By the concession of the Papists themselves, who acknowledge that the church only declares the Scriptures to be authentic, but doth not make it so.[5]

Earlier in this same sermon on the authority of Scripture he stated, "The preaching of the truth, or writing it, makes no difference; but still is the same truth, which is the foundation of the church, whether it be written or preached."[6] The Scriptures contained the truth of God, and it was the truth of God that built the church. Therefore, Owen naturally connected teaching and heralding the word of God being the very essence of true preaching. He expected from these writings for pastors to come to the pulpit well-studied and prepared to convey what the word really said. To be considered preaching in Owen's thought pattern, it must be in line with the truth of the Scriptures for only the Scriptures provide the church with its foundation.

Remember what Paul told Timothy in 2 Tim 2:15 whereby he stated, "Be diligent to present yourself approved to God as a workman who does not need to be ashamed, accurately handling the word of truth." Paul commands Timothy, a pastor, to "be diligent," "accurately handling the word of truth." One commentator puts it this way:

5. Owen, *Works*, 8:513.
6. Owen, *Works*, 8:509.

"Be Diligent" refers to a person being zealous or eager. Timothy must put forth every effort to be a Christian minister approved by God. When his work is inspected by God, he will then have no reason to feel ashamed. "Who correctly handles" suggests a plowman making a straight furrow in the soil. As Timothy teaches the Scriptures, *he is to guide the word of truth along a straight path* and not turn aside into the devious paths of deceiving interpretations.[7]

This assessment by Paul seems to be at the heart of Owen's recorded ideology of sermon preparation per his writings. The laborious study of the Scriptures to rightly present the truth is something that a pastor is to do in approaching the text he is to preach that Lord's Day. Owen, in his book *True Nature of a Gospel Church*, charged that it was the pastor's duty to study rightly the word and come forth what God has really said in the Bible. For Owen, the pastor was to interpret the Bible correctly and studying it with great effort. To do this, pastors must be equipped through proper study and preparation. Owen stated that a pastor and teacher is required to have:

> A clear, sound, comprehensive knowledge of the entire doctrine of the gospel, attained by all means useful and commonly prescribed unto that end, especially by diligent study of the Scripture, with fervent prayer for illumination and understanding. Men cannot preserve for others which they are ignorant of themselves.[8]

Owen here called pastors to labor in intensive study. He would, according to this quote, seemingly have agreed with the modern day standard hermeneutic textbook written by Fee and Stuart on the role of the student of the word being "to attempt to hear the word as the original recipients were to have heard it, to find out what was the original intent of the words of the Bible."[9]

---

7. Barker, *Expositor's Bible Commentary*, 912. Emphasis mine.

8. Owen, *True Nature of a Gospel Church*, 82.

9. Fee and Stuart, *How to Read the Bible*, 27.

Owen seemed to understand that per 2 Tim 2:15 the pastoral preaching of a man must match what the word really taught. He went on to write about the role of a pastor being to enlarge the kingdom of Christ, which he stated comes from the principal cause God has ordained to use, namely, the preaching of the word. Owen states, "Now, the principal instrumental cause of all these is the preaching of the word; and this is committed unto the pastors of the churches."[10] John Owen saw the correct exposition of Scripture and the proclamation of the truth of the gospel having in it the effect of converting those lost sheep out of the world and edifying the church of God.[11] A pastor, per Owen, was to "'*labour* in the word and doctrine,' 1 Tim. V. 17; and thereby to 'feed the flock over which the Holy Ghost hath made them overseers,' and it is that which is everywhere given them in charge."[12] He clearly saw that pastors were to spend their time in studying and laboring over the right interpretation of Scripture in order to present the truths of Scripture in sermons to bear upon the minds, wills, and affections of those who were entrusted to their care. This was preaching for John Owen. That is to know the Scripture rightly and to herald in such a way that those in an attendance who were of Christ would grow in the faith and those not of Christ may be converted. Owen lamented the downgrade in studied and faithful preaching during his time. He wrote, "we have lived to see and hear of reproachful scorn and contempt cast upon laborious preaching,—that is 'labouring in the word and doctrine,'—and all manner of discouragements given unto it."[13] The importance of pastors knowing the Bible, studying the Bible, explaining the Bible rightly, and presenting the truths of the Bible to bear on the consciences of men was scorned, per Owen, in his time. He saw this as a direct assault at the very means that God decreed to use to create a true gospel church.

10. Owen, *Works*, 16:83.

11. Owen, *Works*, 16:80.

12. Owen, *Works*, 16:75.

13. Owen, *Works*, 16:75.

Must Be Skilled in the Study of Scripture

Earlier in this book we analyzed how Owen saw the pastor's competence to preach as vitally important for the pastor to be able to perform his function in the life of the local church. It is helpful in defining Owen's understanding of pastoral preaching in light of Scripture to return to that for a moment. Owen in his writings seems to have believed that a true faithful pastor would have the skill required to divide the word of God rightly. He wrote in *True Nature of a Gospel Church*:

> Skill to divide the word aright, 2 Tim ii. 15; and this consists in a practical wisdom, upon a diligent attendance unto the word of truth, to find out what is real, substantial, and meet food for the souls of the hearers,—to give unto all sorts of person in the church that which is their proper portion.[14]

Owen was not for an untrained pastoral ministry. Though a dissenter, he believed preaching pastors must have the "skill" to study the Bible rightly and convey the truth correctly. Owen upheld that a pastor must have the ability to interpret Scripture and the fervent dedication to do the work required to pull forth the truth from Holy Scripture for the flock of Christ.

For Owen a pastor had to give the proper time to fill their minds with the Scripture in intense thought to find out what the Scripture really conveyed and then prepare to present his discovery in a way that would be clear to the hearers. This is the very essence of Owen's preaching ideology as seen from his statements. A pastor studies the Scripture to uncover the truth of the text then prepares a message from the Scripture rightly understood for an audience in real time with real-life issues. Owen demanded that a pastor exegetically examine the Scripture, pull out its meaning, and present that to the flock for them to feast upon and for those in attendance to wrestle with if they were unconverted.

14. Owen, *Works*, 16:76.

Do Not Forget Application

However, just knowing the meaning was not where Owen believed a pastor should stop in his sermon. Peter tells the elders in 1 Pet 5:2 to shepherd the flocks amongst them. They were to know the recipients of pastoral preaching struggles and situations to better take the truth of Scripture and apply it to them. Owen seemingly conveyed that very thought in his book *True Nature of a Gospel Church*:

> A prudent and diligent consideration of the state of the flock over which any man is set, as unto their strength or weaknesses, their growth or defect in knowledge (the measure of their attainments requiring either milk or strong meat), their temptations and duties, their spiritual decays or thrivings; and that not only in general, but, as near as may be, with respect unto all the individual members of the church. Without a due regard unto these things, men preach at random, uncertainly fighting, like those that beat the air. Preaching sermons not designed for the advantage of them to whom they are preached; insisting on general doctrines not levelled to the condition of the auditory; speaking what men can, without consideration of what they ought,—are things that will make men weary of preaching, when their minds are not influenced with outward advantages, as much as make others weary in hearing them.[15]

Here we see that for John Owen a lack of understanding of the flock under a pastor's charge would produce preaching that, while truthful, lacked the pointed application required by faithful stewards of the Word. This ideology seems to square with what we find in 1 Pet 5:1–5. Owen, in his book *True Nature of a Gospel Church*, conveyed the importance of proper application of the truth to the flock of Christ.[16] He required that pastors not only study the word of God but also know and study the state of those entrusted to their care.[17] He demanded that pastors study their flocks. He did not

15. Owen, *Works*, 16:76–77.

16. Owen, *Works*, 16:76–77.

17. Owen, *Works*, 16:76–77.

think pastors were to stop at just getting the text right. That was step one. The next step was to apply those truths to the very lives and situations of that particular local church.[18] John Owen saw faithful preaching as no less than the proper explanation and proclamation of Scripture, yet to stop there would be to fall short of the mark: faithful pastoral preaching.[19] A pastor was to preach to the church with the condition of the recipients in mind. Application of the truths uncovered in Scripture were to be clear. A person was not to walk away from the local church gathering without knowing clearly how the truth of Holy Scripture applied to them in their daily toil.[20] A pastor must know his flock well to be able to engage their life situations, struggles, temptations, temperaments, etc., with the clear truths of Scripture. Anything less Owen saw as preaching that simply "beat the air."[21]

John Owen held the position clearly, from his writings, that pastoral preaching was the correct reading, exposition, explanation, and application of Scripture to a particular flock from a pastor who knew that flock's circumstances, situations, struggles, and standings well. He demanded that pastors of his time study their flock and knew them well so that they would appropriately apply the truths of Scripture to them in their context for their growth in Christ.[22] From our analysis it appears clear that Owen's comprehensive view of pastoral preaching is rooted in the ideology we find in texts like 1 Pet 5, 2 Tim 2:15, and 2 Tim 3:16—4:5. Owen, in the vein of biblical thought, viewed preaching as a labor of diligence and faithfulness unto God for the good of a local flock.

18. Owen, *Works*, 16:76–77.

19. Owen, *Works*, 16:76–77.

20. Owen, *Works*, 16:76–77.

21. Owen, *Works*, 16:76–77.

22. Owen, *Works*, 16:76–77.

Conclusion: The Biblical Imperative of Pastoral Preaching

How does John Owen's view of pastoral preaching compare to the Word of God's view of preaching? Was Owen faithful to the Scriptures' admonitions and example in this area? The word translated *"preach"* in 2 Timothy 4:2 is the word *kēryssō* and means "to herald," "to proclaim." It is a verb in the imperative mood, active voice, which means Paul is commanding Timothy to carry this out. The Greek word *kēryssō* carried with it the concept of proclaiming a message on behalf of another. Timothy is to herald the good news of the Scriptures on behalf of his King, the Lord Jesus, to all those in his church. The audience in view in 2 Tim 4:1–5 is clearly the professing church as seen in Paul's statement about their forsaking doctrine for that which tickles their eyes in verse 3–4 and separating evangelism from his other ministerial duties (preaching) in verse 5. Therefore, this preaching that Timothy was to engage in was a heralding of the truth of Scripture to the flock of Christ he had been entrusted with as a steward of the Lord Jesus Christ. The goal was for the flock of Christ to gaze upon the Lord Jesus from the word and know him. Edwards highlights the aim of the doctrines found in Holy Scripture when he wrote:

> The doctrines I speak of are those Christians living by
> faith, not by sight; their giving glory to God, *by trusting*
> *him in the dark; living upon Christ,* and not upon experi-
> ences; not making their good frames the foundation of

their faith; which are excellent and important doctrines indeed.[1]

The pastor, per Edwards and Owen before him (as we have examined in comparison to Scripture), preached the truth of the word of God so that the flock would live upon Christ Jesus. Owen's understanding of pastoral preaching, its recipients, and its priority as examined in this book seems to carry with it the weight Paul gives it in 2 Tim 4:1–2 as well as the plethora of other Scriptural texts mentioned like 2 Tim 2:15; 1 Pet 5:1–5; Eph 4:11–16; etc.

The "Preach the Word" Imperative?

We know from 2 Tim 3:16 that Scripture is what God has ordained to mature his people in the faith. Second Tim 3:16–17 is the Scripture that directly precedes Paul's imperative to Timothy of "preach the word" and answers the question "why preach the word." Paul told Timothy that the Scriptures were inspired by God, God-breathed. They were profitable for teaching the people the truths of God, training in the faith, maturing in Christlikeness, and equipping the people of God for every good work. Reading the Scripture and hearing the Scripture preached is a means of grace. Owen wrote in *The Nature and Cause of Apostasy* that "Gospel truth is the only root whereon gospel holiness will grow."[2] The preaching of the gospel faithfully from the word not only bring sinners to Christ, in Owen's thought, but grew them in Christlike holiness. Owen, though accused by some of being a prophetic political idealist even in the pulpit, conveys in his writings and pastoral sermons a different view of pastoral preaching, one rooted in what we find in the Holy Scripture concerning the office of pastor and the task of preaching. John Owen's pastoral preaching may have included political overtures from time to time, but his writings on pastoral preaching did not convey political idealism as the driving factor of pastoral work. The one thing a pastor cannot fail at in his ministry, per a summation of John Owen's writings on the subject, is to faithfully preach

1. Edwards, *Religious Affections*, 175. Emphasis mine.
2. Owen, *Works*, 7:188.

the word of God to the people of God. He understood that the church of God's well-being was dependent on the faithful preaching of the word of God. For remember Owen's emphasis in this when he wrote, "The first principle duty of a pastor is to feed the flock by diligent preaching of the Word."[3] This matches Paul's exhortation to Timothy in 2 Tim 4:2, "preach the word." Owen, in the vein of thought we see from Scripture, demanded that pastors give all of themselves to this task. He wrote,

> A man is a pastor unto them whom he feeds by pastoral teaching, and to no more. . . . Nor is required only that he preach now and then at his leisure, but that he lay aside all other employments, though lawful, all other duties in the church, as unto such a constant attendance on them as would divert him from his work, that he give himself unto it, that he be in these things labouring to the utmost of his ability.[4]

A pastor, per John Owen, was to give no less than the utmost diligence and effort they could muster to properly interpret and present the truths found in the pages of the Holy Scripture for the spiritual good of the local church. Lewis Allen in his book for pastors called *The Preacher's Catechism* stated God's design for the office of pastor in a way that beautifully summarizes the Scriptural call of pastoral preaching (which we have seen Owen uphold and promote in his writings), "God designs that his church be served by Word-soaked, joy-seeking, and joy-sharing preachers of his delightful gospel. He purposes that those same preachers be mastered by His Word."[5]

Preaching the word is a means of grace to the people of God. Faithful exposition and application of the Holy Scriptures is a blessing to the flock of Christ. For John Owen, there was nothing better to give his life to for the glory of his Shepherd King. For the pastor today, the biblical call heeded by Owen and expounded by him in his writings as examined in this book goes forward. The call to

3. Owen, *Works*, 16:74.
4. Owen, *Works*, 16:74.
5. Allen, *Preacher's Catechism*, 34.

pastors of the church of Lord Jesus is clear. Preach the word! Read, explain, expound, apply, and herald the Holy Scripture for the salvation of sinners and upbuilding of the Lord Jesus' church. Perhaps the LORD would grant the church more pastors who repeat the history of men like John Owen to the praise of his glorious grace.

Bibliography

Allen, Lewis. *The Preacher's Catechism*. Wheaton, IL: Crossway, 2018.

Barker, K. L. *Expositor's Bible Commentary*. Abridged Edition: New Testament. Grand Rapids, MI: Zondervan, 1994.

Barrett, Matthew. "Who Is John Owen?" *Credo: The Prince of Puritans: John Owen* 5.4 (2015) 12–13.

Barret, Matthew, and Michael A. G. Haykin. *Owen on the Christian Life: Living for the Glory of God in Christ*. Wheaton, IL: Crossway, 2015.

Cooper, Tim. *John Owen, Richard Baxter and the Formation of Nonconformity*. Burlington, VT: Ashgate, 2011.

Cowan, Martyn Calvin. *John Owen and the Civil War Apocalypse: Preaching, Prophecy, and Politics*. London: Routledge, 2017.

Cross, F. L., and E. A. Livingstone, eds. *The Oxford Dictionary of the Christian Church*. Rev. 3rd ed. Oxford: Oxford University Press, 2005.

Douglas, J. D., and P. W. Comfort, eds. *Who's Who in Christian History*. Wheaton, IL: Tyndale, 1992.

Edwards, Jonathan. *Religious Affections*. Vol. 2 of *The Works of Jonathan Edwards*. Edited by John E. Smith. New Haven, CT: Yale University, 2009.

Elswell, Walter A., ed. *Evangelical Dictionary of Theology*. 2nd ed. Grand Rapids, MI: Baker, 2001.

Fee, Gordon D., and Douglas Stuart. *How to Read the Bible for All Its Worth*. Grand Rapids, MI: Zondervan, 2014.

Ferguson, Sinclair B. *The Trinitarian Devotion of John Owen*. Orlando, FL: Reformation Trust, 2014.

Gribben, Crawford. *John Owen and English Puritanism*. New York: Oxford University Press, 2016.

Grudem, Wayne. *Systematic Theology: An Introduction to Biblical Doctrine*. 1994. Reprint, Leicester: InterVarsity, 2007.

Jones, Martyn Lloyd. *Preaching and Preachers*. London: Hodder & Stoughton, 1971.

Kapic, Kelly M. "John Owen and the Civil War Apocalypse: Preaching, Prophecy, and Politics." *Church History* 87.3 (2018) 904–7.

Bibliography

Kelly, Ryan. "Reformed or Reforming? John Owen and the Complexity of Theological Codification for Mid-Seventeenth-Century England." In *The Ashgate Research Companion to John Owen's Theology*, edited by Kelly M. Kapic and Mark Jones, 3–30. Burlington, VT: Ashgate, 2012.

Owen, John. *The Works of John Owen*. 23 vols. Edited by William H. Goold. London: The Banner of Truth Trust, 1965–91.

Packer, J. I. *A Quest for Godliness: The Puritan Vision of the Christian Life*. Wheaton, IL: Crossway, 1990.

Toon, Peter. *God's Statesman: The Life and Work of John Owen*. Eugene, OR: Wipf & Stock, 1971.

Trueman, Carl R. *John Owen: Reformed Catholic Renaissance Man*. New York: Routledge, 2016.

www.ingramcontent.com/pod-product-compliance
Lightning Source LLC
Chambersburg PA
CBHW070827100426
42813CB00003B/526